To all those who came before me, who squinted through the darkness
so that I could see today. To my nephew, Calvin Eugene Wingfield III,
and all those who will come after me.
—M.A.H.

For Darlie, my dearest treasure
—V.M.

Text copyright © 2024 by Mary Annaïse Heglar
Jacket art and interior illustrations copyright © 2024 by Vivian Mineker

All rights reserved. Published in the United States by Random House Children's Books, a division of Penguin Random House LLC, New York.

Random House and the colophon are registered trademarks of Penguin Random House LLC.

Visit us on the Web!
rhcbooks.com

Educators and librarians, for a variety of teaching tools, visit us at RHTeachersLibrarians.com

Library of Congress Cataloging-in-Publication Data is available upon request.
ISBN 978-0-593-56801-9 (trade) – ISBN 978-0-593-56802-6 (lib. bdg.) – ISBN 978-0-593-56803-3 (ebook)

The artist used Photoshop and Procreate to create the illustrations for this book.
The text of this book is set in 18-point Futura Round.
Interior design by Elizabeth Tardiff

MANUFACTURED IN CHINA
10 9 8 7 6 5 4 3 2 1
First Edition

The World Is Ours to Cherish

A Letter to a Child

By **Mary Annaïse Heglar**

Illustrated by **Vivian Mineker**

Random House 🏠 New York

There is magic all around you.

You can see it when the sun rises in the morning.

You can feel it when the rain falls from the clouds.

There is magic in the way fish are born to swim
and bees are born to fly.

You are part of this magic:

your smile, your laugh, your heartbeat.

This world will always be beautiful.

It will always be magical.

But the world you are growing up in

is so different from the world I knew.

The ocean has more water.

The sky has more storms.

The land has more fire.

I want you to know how much has changed . . .

. . . so you can see how much there is to cherish.

I want you to cherish the fireflies who light the night sky
and the birds who sing to welcome the morning.

I want you to cherish the wind that tickles your cheek
and the rainbow that peeks out from behind the clouds.

Cherish the breeze that cools you on hot days.

Cherish the trees that protect you from the wind.

Cherish the sunshine and
remember it during storms.

All this beauty, all this magic, is yours.

You belong to it and it belongs to you.

Take better care of it than anyone ever has.

The world will never stop changing.

But you will change it, too.

You won't do it alone.

We'll build a whole new world.

Together.

A world where we share each other's joy . . .

. . . and carry each other through pain.

A world where we care for our planet the same way we care for each other. There will be less "you" and "I" and more "we."

We'll build a world where we take the magic we have and use it to make more.

I wrote this book for my nephew, who was born in 2018 in the throes of climate chaos. He now knows me as his crunchy environmentalist aunt, who buys him books about animals and forests and oceans. He doesn't know that each time I have bought him a book, I have wondered how many of these beautiful beings and places would still exist by the time he was old enough to question the world around him. What answers would I have?

Especially in a world in unimaginable transition, we have to make good on our collective responsibility to the next generation. Whether you are a parent or an aunt or uncle or a teacher or cousin or neighbor, these children need all of us, and we need them. Climate change is real and it is here, but all is not lost. We're not too late—we're just in time to build a new world with our children. The world isn't ending—it's beginning again. And we get to shape it.

First Steps for Changing the World

1. **Talk it out:** It may sound oversimplified, but talking about climate change is the first step toward learning what to do. Children may express uncomfortable emotions, like fear and anger, but it's important that you hear and affirm those emotions, because they are valid. Start by asking what they already know—and you may be surprised by how much they've already observed. Then answer their questions as honestly as you can, and promise to learn more together. In these conversations, make sure to acknowledge our uncomfortable climate reality while making room for climate hope.

2. **Grow something:** Show children that they can be a positive force for nature by growing a houseplant, starting a compost bin, or joining a community garden.

3. **Include children in disaster planning:** As you make your evacuation or shelter-in-place plans for events like floods, fires, and storms, give them room to offer suggestions or ask questions. Make sure they understand the rationale behind your household's or school's plans and what the contingency plans are. Above all, make sure they understand that they are safe and not alone.

4. **Show up:** Connect with a local climate-activist group, and show up to rallies. If you are an educator, see if your school can invite local climate activists to speak to your class or if you can partner with them on upcoming actions. These can be helpful places to share with like-minded individuals and to release emotions—as well as to make your voices heard.

5. **Build community:** One of the best ways to build resilience in the face of disaster is to cultivate strong social ties. Get to know your neighbors, join mutual-aid groups, teach kids to look out for their older neighbors, and make it a group activity to check on them. If you work in a school, take students on field trips to local community hubs so they can learn more about the world at their fingertips.